"When Whales Went Back to the Water deftly n
microscopic, geological, and intimate perspectives to show how
we are 'animal[s] made of other animals'—and the grief and
belonging that entails. Amidst housefires, environmental decline,
domestic abuse, the word 'trauma' graffitied on a garbage bin,
Baird conjures hard-earned awe."
    —ADÈLE BARCLAY, author of *Renaissance Normcore*

"When Whales Went Back to the Water sings and pushes
language with its uncanny imagery, unexpected word choices
and combinations, and play with spacing and breath. With its
linguistic lifts, Baird's collection shows the power of free verse
to convey lyric beauty."
    —JENNA BUTLER, author of *Revery: A Year of Bees*

"In *When Whales Went Back to the Water*, Lisa Baird asks us to see
the sacred in each moment. Again and again, this book calls us to
the present with a clear voice and a sharp eye. Personal loss and
collective emergency meet poignant truths of the natural world.
'A relocated coyote will do whatever it takes to get back home,'
Baird tells us. She bares her own path home to herself: past nettle
patches and open fields, through echoing violence and recovery,
to the messy kitchen floor of new parenthood. We are in this
together, these poems remind us. Even solitude is a collective
condition."
    —ALESSANDRA NACCARRATO, author of *Imminent Domains:
    Reckoning with the Anthropocene*

"What gorgeous magic Baird excavates from human circumstance.
Rich with celebration, grief, and a touch of science, *When Whales
Went Back to the Water* navigates a labyrinth of survivals. 'You
will / grow to be a wild thing,' Baird promises. And isn't that the
gift we each most desire?"
    —JEANANN VERLEE, author of *PREY*, *Said the Manic to the Muse*,
    and *Racing Hummingbirds*

WHEN
WHALES
WENT
BACK
TO THE
WATER

LISA BAIRD

WHEN
WHALES
WENT
BACK
TO THE
WATER

UNIVERSITY
of **ALBERTA**
PRESS

Published by

University of Alberta Press
1-16 Rutherford Library South
11204 89 Avenue NW
Edmonton, Alberta, Canada T6G 2J4
amiskwaciwâskahikan | Treaty 6 |
Métis Territory
ualbertapress.ca | uapress@ualberta.ca

**Library and Archives Canada
Cataloguing in Publication**

Title: When whales went back to the
    water / Lisa Baird.
Names: Baird, Lisa, 1979– author
Series: Robert Kroetsch series.
Description: Series statement: Robert
    Kroetsch series
Identifiers: Canadiana (print) 2024048083X |
    Canadiana (ebook) 20240481976 |
    ISBN 9781772127966 (softcover) |
    ISBN 9781772128123 (EPUB) |
    ISBN 9781772128130 (PDF)
Classification: LCC PS8603.A4442 W44
    2025 | DDC C811/.6—dc23

First edition, first printing, 2025.
First printed and bound in Canada by
Houghton Boston Printers, Saskatoon,
Saskatchewan.
Copyediting and proofreading by
Gil Adamson.

A volume in the Robert Kroetsch Series.

University of Alberta Press is committed
to protecting our natural environment.
As part of our efforts, this book is printed
on Enviro Paper: it contains 100% post-
consumer recycled fibres and is acid- and
chlorine-free.

GPSR: Easy Access System Europe |
Mustamäe tee 50, 10621 Tallinn, Estonia |
gpsr.requests@easproject.com

University of Alberta Press gratefully
acknowledges the support received for its
publishing program from the Government
of Canada, the Canada Council for the
Arts, and the Government of Alberta
through the Alberta Media Fund.

Contents

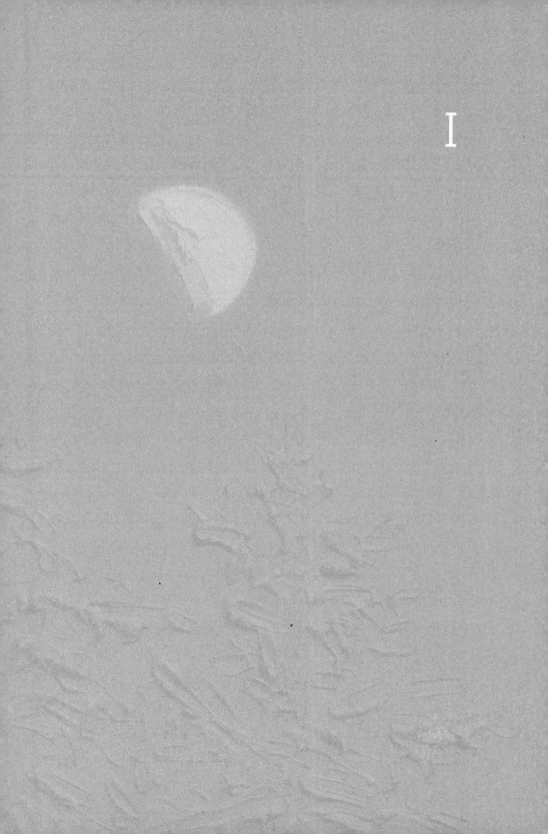

I

When Whales Went Back to the Water

Say life began here in a tidal pool.
Or hot spring. Or where the earth's core

steams through fissures in the ocean floor.
I like that all of these theories are wet.

I like to think of the first animal, born
of chaos and collision, molecules whipping

into cellular form. It is calming
to think about geological time scales.

Whales only took 10 million years to leave
the land and commit to salt water.

Who wouldn't want to sing
to someone 10,000 miles away?

I like that they swam, then walked,
then returned to the water as mammals,

with live births and blowholes, diving deeper
than any other air breather to linger

for hours. I had a story about how quiet
it must be down there, but it's not

anymore. I keep learning things about other people
that I didn't want to know. I've been practising,

but can only hold my breath for three minutes.
It is calming to think about large numbers.

How many trillions of cells there are in me.
Most of them not even human. Dividing,

dying, killing, feeding, excreting.
I feel ok today so I guess enough of them

are cooperating with each other.
The wallpaper on my phone says "tolerate

uncertainty" over a picture of a whale.
I like that I can't see the wrist or finger bones

within its fins. I want to use the word kin
like I've always known what it means,

this body recalling times before topsoil,
bread or algebra, before doorways,

bull kelp, forgetting, or photosynthesis.
To reach back to being eager

and alive as our common ancestor
emerging in the flash and muck

alone, but knowing there would be more.

Poem That Wanted to Be an Apple

Wanted to twist oxygen
and light into flesh, one

of many red bells in the trees,
revered as scholars, or gods.

Poem that wanted to be 25% air,
wanted to glad-haunt

the orchard, the bushel,
the bowl on the table.

Wanted teeth on skin,
that good pain—gnawed

to a tight constellation of seeds,
dark database exposed.

Poem that wanted to be
known, to be necessary,

to rest in the palm
of your hand.

It Is Relevant That I'm Ovulating

I ride a cocktail of endogenous drugs with a loose laugh
and heavy hand with eyeshadow, thighs hips and belly pressing

warm grass by the bridge spanning the Speed River
just as it rushes into the Eramosa, propped up on my elbows

responding to texts, by which I mean
not avoiding the rivers or the trees but sending love

notes to everyone who hasn't heard back from me
in the last month: *I'm still here, I'm glad you are too. By the way,*

someone cared enough to make little wooden
shelters for all the snapping turtle nests by the parking lot!

A friend arrives with his partner and because I adore my friend
I plan to love his partner too, as well as their dog,

who yanks on the leash as we discuss a documentary they've just seen
until a slight movement to my right grabs my attention

and I windmill my arms come-here-come-here
as I chant, *OH my god OH my god OH my god*

at a pair of eastern garter snakes coiling a figure eight,
inches from my feet. They twist back into the undergrowth

and we wonder aloud whether they are mating,
since spring is long gone, or just making out—do snakes make out?

I remember my first time, nervous and elated
arriving at life drawing class, stepping out of my boots and blurting

Is she wearing a real snake? The nude model with a friend
draped long and heavy over her shoulders,

hugging her neck. During the tea break, the snake
slid off, reappearing in the oven, which was not on at the time.

I asked the model (I might not have slept that night
if I hadn't) *I've heard that reptiles don't feel or express*

affection because they don't have limbic brains,
is that true? She shook her head emphatically no,

said the snake was as tender as any of her cats.
I tell my friends this, wanting to linger in the invitation

of snake bodies inscribing infinity on warm dirt,
no beginning, no end, like they opened a world outside of time

and allowed our rushing in, like we learned
a new language for an instant and it was ardent and necessary,

like I could call this holy, and no one would laugh.

Explanation

for Dave

The sum of the world's online
data in 2018 was 33 zettabytes
which, despite sounding like
a school of tropical fish, is a huge
number, and while *saving to cloud*
sounds cool, moist, and easy,
like our data simply swims
above us, I only recently
registered that of course, the whole
of the internet—the contents
of your draft folders in all three
email accounts, the photo
of the 1,400-year-old
gingko tree with a hallelujah
of yellow leaves, every Bitcoin
transaction, DIY plumbing video,
and dormant LinkedIn profile—
is captured in warehouses
that are called server farms,
although they grow nothing,
being arid corridors
lined with millions of racks
of computers and backup
computers, the hum and exhale
of which is soothed
by innumerable fans,
whirring, dogged, while
the less energy-intensive
methods of preventing
meltdown of precious
machinery require water
in amounts that Google
will not disclose, all of which

forms an argument for sending
fewer emails and writing
things on paper—which, yes,
is also complicated!—but
while I know the futility
of individual solutions
to global problems, still,
tonight when I pause mid-
fold by the laundry basket
as you begin to undress
before bed, it's because
I'm picturing the next
poem written in slow
cursive with a rain-wet
fingertip across
the small of your back.

The Biggest Disappointment of My 16th Year

I lean against the wood panelling, crossing and uncrossing my arms in the dimly lit hall at the Legion in Kingston at my first Womyn's Dance. The two friends who talked me into coming tonight are slow dancing to Indigo Girls' "Power of Two." A whole room of women laughing, flirting. I stare. Resolve to stop staring. Women's fingers on cold wet beer bottles. Women's bodies pressed together in the smoky haze. My hair is too long, these men's wool trousers are scratchy and hot, my underwear clings to sweaty skin and I can't decide what to do with my hands.

Square shoulders, heavy black boots. My body responds to the tall lean form in a dress shirt and tie striding past me. The jawline, the flash of teeth as they grin and wave to someone on the other side of the dance floor. I inhale sharply at an urgent uncoiling heat, my body understanding something it hadn't before. But I won't hear the words *butch, transmasculine* or *genderfuck* for years. I take a lurching step forward as someone hands them a beer, then halt, face burning. Blink back tears. *Am I straight after all?* A fast song starts. My two friends keep slow dancing.

She Says, *I don't think I'm going to fall for you*

but still wants to be lovers. I don't know how to do that,
so we only ever kiss—outside my apartment building

in the winter rains, beneath cherry trees in April.
She murmurs something like

I want to tear you up right now,
against a hallway wall at a party.

One day while we speak, I follow fragments
of childhood memories leading

like crumbs or knives to a picture waiting
at the bottom of my mind,

n understanding that makes me buckle and shake
as shattered pieces of myself come back together.

She laughs softly because that's how she copes,
and holds me close. She doesn't doubt me.

Another time she describes standing in the yard
as a kid and watching something dark,

furred and slow, broader than the family car
with curving tusks. The heave

of its breath as it lumbers past.
She offers no explanation, only certainty

of what she saw, and while I look for her
after losing touch, I just find one mention

of a dance performance in the Yukon.
I still believe you, Judith.

An Alternate Universe in Which My Trauma Response
Is Made of Birds

A startle of sparrows
launching from the branch
to fly into a window again,
or the fatigue of grackles circling
with nowhere to land. A sharpness
of hummingbirds tearing into
one another, needle-beaked.
That cardinal pecking
at its reflection until glass shatters.
An immobility of meadowlarks
unblinking in tall grass. I am
an animal made of other animals,
their tiny hammering hearts
orbiting the moment that something
breaks, something survives
and something else moves just as fast
as its shadow.

Time Machine

Adults didn't notice the half-inch
gap between my feet and the floor,
the clean soles of my shoes
or the dry burden of dread crushing
the air. It wasn't a conscious choice
to unlatch, to hover just above.
I slipped out of rooms in silence.
I stared at books or out a window,
safe and quiet as a pinned moth—how
would I know to want anything else?

Give me a time machine. I'll peer
through a blur of red to find the egg
that becomes me, a soft jewel
inside my mother's mother. I'll set
it on a fingertip, wet and intact, raise
it up to the light, repeat *You will
grow to be a wild thing* until we both
believe it.

The Day Dad Starts Hitting My Younger Brother

and I am the one to tell Mom,
she shrinks, folds over at the dining room table.
Cradles her head in her hands—
a heavy, aching egg.
She sways side to side like a metronome:
I can't handle this I can't handle this

until her body starts to blur,
the slat-backed chair visible
through her cloudy torso.
I practise holding my breath
so as not to blow the last
of her away.

The First Time I Go Skinny-Dipping

Tracy, Amy, and I strip quickly in the dark. Dive off the dock, stroke towards the centre of a small lake in northern Ontario. I float on my back, gape at an impossibility of stars. *I feel so free. Do you feel it?* we ask each other. Just the slip and lift of the lake.

The first time I go skinny-dipping, bra size is a different planet, shaving ceases to exist, this wholly new body belonging only to me, to the water.

The first time I go skinny-dipping, Laila steals our clothes and towels, her grin lit by the fire while we shiver on the dock shouting threats. The other girls drape their hair in front of their breasts, run trying to cover themselves before snatching up towels. I stride up last, swinging arms by my sides as if I don't give a damn who sees. Lean in to give Laila an eyeful of tightened, dripping nipples, and say *I'll get you for that.* She answers easily *Oh, I'm scared.* Neither of us looks away.

In Defence of Purple

The colour of Disney villains
and the soft fist of your spleen.

Named for shellfish boiled
for days to make dye.

The grape hyacinth raising
a constellation of phalluses

above mid-May snow. Not
Easter eggs or the walls

of a grade-schooler's bedroom.
Rather, a Crown Royal bag

heavy with marbles. Purple
as seventh and last in line, the most

ultra wavelength. As culmination.
Which is to say, survivor.

The scapegoat refusing to hide
bruises or hickeys. Could

have told me at 11 to quit
dabbing concealer under my eyes

where the thinnest skin shows
everyone everything. Which

is why, before leaving, I wrote
my name in purple sharpie

on the walls. And why, come July,
I'll be deep in the blackberries—

forearms crosshatched in blood,
teeth and tongue dark as eggplant,

as plum, as hunger.

Poem That Wanted to Be an Icicle

Wanted the return of its strangest names.
Ickel, eckel. Ice-candle.

Wanted to be hollow, flutelike,
also twisted, gnarled.

Wanted to capture light and not let it go.
To confound physicists, to be a problem

like black hole information paradox
or the identity of dark matter.

Wanted to be its own creature.
Long-stemmed, or squat and forked.

To be read and reread,
resisting translation.

Wanted to absorb the warmth
of your attention and melt

and freeze at the same time,
to weave itself of flows of water

and air and latent heat.
Morphologically unstable,

dynamically wet, like ink running off a page.
Wanted to form during a storm

off the side of the bird feeder,
high winds pushing droplets

sideways and up to the ever-extending
tip, to grow at an uncanny angle

a bright spear aiming its fierce will at the sky.

She Says It's Dangerous to Open Umbrellas Indoors

When it starts to rain inside,
      you stop having anyone over.

                You're not allowed to call the landlord.
          She doesn't trust plumbers.

The carpet squelches underfoot.
      Your heels blister from rubber boots.

          She won't go outside.
                It'll just be grey out there too.

          You bring her sunflowers
             and she accuses you of cheating.

        You hoard coins for the dryer,
smuggle clothes to the laundry room

when you want to visit a friend.
      Until you find a note taped

        to your jar of quarters.
          What if I drowned while you were out.

      The neighbours step around the wet patch
        by the door to your apartment.

One of them catches your eye, says,
    If you ever want to talk.

      You empty the bottom shelves and drawers.
Black mould speckles the walls.

She sees something moving
        in the water and refuses to leave the bed.

                        You lie awake at night as the toilet struggles
                to keep emptying.

                One morning, before the water level rose higher
        than the edge of the tub, you poured

a bath, soaked in hot water
        with raindrops sparkling your lashes.

                        It rained harder, stinging your scalp
                                and shoulders, cooling the bath.

                Lying back with everything
        but your face underwater you thought

        if you were patient, if you looked hard
                enough, you'd see some blue peeking through.

Why I Thought Dating Women Would Be Safer

When I'm 12, I start
to question things.
Like why Dad doesn't want
Mom to go practice
with her folk band.
When he's lounging in his chair,
loosened by wine and willing
to explain the world, I ask.
He tells me he thinks my mother
is *deee*lectable, so it follows
that someone else would
also find her *deee*lectable
and we can't have her parking
in some underground lot.
Anyone could help themselves
to what's not theirs.
And he leans over to refill my glass.

On Seeing the Word Trauma Graffitied on a Garbage Bin

The trees and I with our long-legged shadows.
The play structures edged in gold. And the wound

I keep picking, busy with my stubborn animal
anger, the way I cradle rage when someone wrongs me,

tend it like a garden upon which survival depends, still an addict,
17 years sober but hooked on the stress hormones telling righteousness

to my blood and I know how addiction reshapes the brain,
my neurons' dendrites permanently elongated

anticipating anger with a bleak, elastic glee, and I want it to stop,
which is why I'm in a park in December at an hour past dawn

pacing and talking to myself until whatever subtle or unsubtle
offering arrives—something will happen, it always does—

like when just seconds before I say out loud
to an indifferent squirrel, *Trauma is garbage!* an arm

thrusts through an opening from another dimension and a hand scrawls
in aquamarine the word that will make me sit down

on the cold gravel path in front of a grey garbage bin,
the vapour of my astonished breath the only movement

for miles around.

The Mouth Is Your Hardest and Softest Place

The salivary glands
release a litre of saliva each day.

Seventy-two strains
of bacteria grow there.

The estrogen surge at ovulation
makes crystals in saliva

in the shape of ferns.
A forest floor under

the tongue, visible
by microscope. It's called

ferning. Proteins in saliva
stimulate the growth

of blood vessels.
It's why we lick

our wounds. Enzymes
in saliva can kill sperm.

Rock scissors paper,
rock saliva sperm.

Salivary gland stones
grow like mutant teeth

or claws or tiny coffins,
blocking the flow

of saliva in a mouth
repeatedly forced

to swallow. The dry
mouth is a stalled verb.

The dry tongue can't
taste anything, can't tend

its wounds or scream
its way out of the woods.

Enzymes in saliva
prevent bloodstains

from setting. Saliva conquers
blood. Rock saliva blood.

All our sheets, still white.

Blue Angel

My dad, nearly 50 and over 6 feet tall, bends down to grasp the
bar at the back of my Blue Angel banana seat bike—which I chose
at Canadian Tire because it is blue and not pink—and holds me
upright, running up and down the block in the summer heat.
(Was it a string of sun-drunk afternoons? Only an hour?) He runs
till he doesn't, and maybe he's just chest-heaving tired, but I
want to believe that he knows the moment my centre of gravity
finds the sweet spot—when my arms, legs, spine, and cerebellum
align—and this man who has never let anything go in his life
lets go, and I remain upright, pedalling away from him while he
beams with relief but maybe, I want to believe, also pride as the
cicadas keen and I am perfect physics and perfect trust, flying.

Ode to the Mississauga Women's Clinic

The low lighting in the waiting room where we sit,
faces lit by phones or staring at the opposite wall.
The receptionist with a soft voice and quick facts.
The friend who leaves work in the middle
of the day to accompany me. The staff
who explain the pills, the nurse who draws
the blood. A smaller second waiting room,
just me and a woman with blonde hair tugging
the blue paper gown over her knees.

Are you nervous, I ask. *Yes,* says Christina,
not her real name, and talks about the three-
year-old son she's raising on her own,
her lousy ex, the family doctor who refused
to refer her until she was 13 weeks along.
I'm 40, I tell her, *I still can't believe this happened.*
You do not look 40, she says, which is what women
in their thirties say to women in their forties
when they want to say *Thank you.*

Skullcap tincture and ginger tea. Ibuprofen
and Tylenol. Seven hours of tissue tearing
loose. Contractions every 5 seconds
as organs grip and push. The 14 years
of meditation and the second season
of *Good Girls* that make breathing possible.

Beth fucks Rio, this time in her and Dean's bed.
Suck in air, count to 5, push air out.
Annie and Ruby almost rob a bank.
Suck in air, count to 5, push air out.

The heave and the hot spill. Resting
the head on the toilet seat and the moan.
The small relief of making a sound. The tremble
and sweat. The abiding body, for how could
this be anything other than an ode to the body,
still shedding, still coming apart, still whole.

II

All His Ex-Girlfriends Are Monstrous

It's lucky I didn't end up in jail.
Never have you felt such tenderness

as when you heard what he did
to the last girlfriend.

He holds nothing back. The ex who
stopped touching him. Then left.

The ex who read his journal and stole
his cats. The ex who flaunted a new lover.

You revel in the obvious—
you are not like them.

*I needed you to hear this
from me.* How your eyes burn

as you press his hand between yours.
How you are passing every test.

Affirming Femme

It won't always be so hard.
This is just a raw time.

Once I'm passing,
he reminds you, *it'll be ok.*

He's so tender, post-rage.
Praises you with his hands

like you are something bruised
and holy. There's always

a reason. A bad night's sleep.
The ulcers. His jealousy.

He's working on it. Once
he's passing, it'll be ok.

And you'll pass as the straight
girl on his arm. No one's

talking about that part. But
you understand. None of this

is about you.

You Don't Understand

that he wants to polish your jealousy
like a favourite pair of boots.

You reach out to the flirt
who wrote him that poem,

thinking he'll be pleased. He screams,
Get out or I'm gonna hurt you.

You run until your breath knifes
your throat and you crumple

in the high school parking lot.
When you return that night your bed

is a wet flower, the duvet
dark with blood and he is curled,

foetal, wailing. *Sorry I was bad.*
A child fearful of a raised fist.

You pull him close, clean
and bandage his forearms.

Certain again of what is expected
of you.

You Could Have Said Something

Let's go for a walk instead, the sun is finally out

He pushes you back down, buries
his face between your legs.

I'm actually getting a bit bored

He wrings another climax from your body.

I want to get out of bed now

Grabs your wrist when you reach for your jeans.

I'm sore

It happens again.

no

All day.

You Leave the House for Three Different Reasons

The chiropractor—your hip is wrecked.
Therapy, which he says he's fine with.

And school. You're always late.
It's hard to get out the door in the morning,

hard to slice an apple or pour tea
with the flat stare from the couch

whenever you're about to leave him
home alone. You open and close the fridge,

unable to find your lunch. Misplace
your bike helmet. Stand in the apartment hallway

weighing whether it's worth going back in
for your textbook. You overhear him on the phone

with his mom: *Lisa seems anxious in the mornings,*
and you're touched that he noticed,

that he cares.

At the End of the Visit

You offer your new friend a ride home—
her house is two bus rides away,
and you're enjoying the conversation.
He rips the car key from your hand.
Ignores stop signs. Swerves
between lanes, steps on the gas
like there's a neck under his foot.

You stare down at your twisting
hands, and know a cool rush
of relief when the car jerks to a halt
and your friend climbs out
saying only *Thanks*

for dropping me off.

Near the End

A spiral-bound sketchbook with a
black ribbon to mark the pages.
You've never actually drawn
in it. But his first night in the
hospital—the first time you're
alone in a year and a half—
something else guides your
hand.

Blooms and leaves jungle
from the margins, swallow to-dos
and grocery lists.

At his bedside, offering toast, tea
and comics, you show him your
drawings. *I guess you're happier
without me around.* You duck out
to sob in the washroom again,
stop at the kitchenette to heat
him some broth. Still carrying
the sketchbook—proof

of something.

The Night You Break Up He Regresses Again

You know the sound of an infant's acute distress.
Whimpering, loud sobbing,

then a wail, high, flat, and nasal.
He won't remember

what his body does tonight,
and you won't speak of it.

You, watching it all from above, floating
by a light fixture, while in bed, your limbs

and torso form a container
for his thrashing

as what you knew would happen
is happening again,

for the last time.

How to Win after Leaving

Delete the voicemail before the end. Win.

Burn the letter. Smear the ash into the sidewalk. Win.

No, save the letter for the restraining order. Lose.

Decide against filing the police report. Cops are transphobic already. Lose.

File it after all. Feel worse. Lose.

Order pizza. Panic at the doorbell. Lose.

Forget to close the curtains the day he watches from across the street. Lose.

Drink enough to pretend not to care that he stares at you in the gay bar. Win

Pretend not to care so well you convince yourself. Win.

Tongue kiss your friends on the dance floor. Win win win.

Find out that he's fucking your new roommate. Lose.

Get a different roommate. Win, sort of.

Get work in a location so remote that food and mail arrive via helicopter. Win

Fall in love with someone new. Win. Move to Manchester. Win.

Tell friends what happened. Win. Tell friends what happened. Lose.

Go three years without hearing from him. Win. Four years. Five. Seventeen.

III

If You Sing It Slowly Enough

Slow laps in the dark. Eight steps from the fridge to the table.
Fourteen to the couch. Past the recycling bin, back to the fridge.

The baby strapped to your torso knocks her forehead
against the bruise on your collarbone, chirps, bounces.

Whips her head around to peer out the window as you walk past.
If you sing it slowly enough, any song is a lullaby.

Later, you'll sob on the couch between loops. The clock
on the stove, covered with a dishcloth. You don't want to know.

Also, blue light, wakefulness. Something about shorter
wavelength and melatonin production, the pineal gland

withholding the building blocks of sleep. Does an infant's body
remember a time before artificial lighting? Before factory jobs

ate all the hours and we slept twice each night? First sleep
at dusk, then second sleep. An hour or two in the middle

for sex, poetry, prayer. Is there a patron saint of melatonin?
You are praying to the goddess of sleep to tuck you both

under her dim wing. All hail sleep and these holy hours
while we pursue it, wearing through carpet despite the tremble

in the calves, the ache of the trapezius, the warm 20 lb. weight
of the child who cannot settle, this ungodly child who won't sleep.

Is it her asthma medication? The modem blinking in the corner?
Did you get her outside enough today? How will you carry her

like this when she's two or three? At least one experiment
by scientists who seem to hate rats suggests that sleep

deprivation can kill. Hallucinations. Sections of the brain
degenerating. Organ shutdown. The cradle will fall. So many

lullabies about death. Tomorrow your mind will wrap itself
in gauze, but don't think of that now. Don't look at the clock.

Where's the wormhole to an alternate universe where clocks
were never invented? If you walk in circles long enough

can you step through to the lost hours of sleep? There they are,
the hours processing with girlfriends in your twenties,

scrolling after Trump was elected, after Doug Ford, when you thought
you ordered decaf but didn't, were going to nap but caught up

on email instead. The hours, the nights, the years' worth
of lost sleep lined up deep and wide like good pillows.

And here, the goddess of sleep presides on a queen-sized mattress
in a checked flannel gown with chamomile and valerian

winding through her tattoos. She takes you into her arms
and whispers, *If you sing it slowly enough—*

Start with an Ode to the Toddler's Lung Capacity

To the decibel range, uninhibited diaphragm,
and sense of timing. How she waits till you arrive

in the tiny tinny bathroom for a diaper change
to slam the door, pivot, look you in the eye and carve

you open with sound. Write another, to not stepping on
her voice with yours, saying instead *Let's not fight,*

and the ways you both grope for control in the weeks
after her Oma's stroke. Include the coldest nights

of Ottawa winter, an emergency stay-at-home order,
the flooded basement, that scheduler at the personal

support worker company who keeps promising
We'll send help next week, and the stacks

of plastic takeout containers and casserole dishes
from friends who pause at the bottom

of the front steps. *If there's anything else I can do.*
If it weren't for the pandemic I'd—

Write several poems to the bathmat's
imprint on the left side of your face,

and the phrases she repeats—*Mama cried*
on the bathroom floor or *Oma died* or

Oma's dead. The '90s Björk she belts
while stirring oatmeal onto the table, into her lap,

the library parking lot with the snow
mountain, the demand that you tickle her

through her snowsuit, endorphins
wheeling like headless reindeer.

Write an epic of not knowing. Of saying again
We're definitely going home, we just don't know when,

and the final time her Oma says *Bring the dear child here,*
and strokes her granddaughter's curls with her good arm.

Tell it all, that you tend the family ghosts by never hitting
the children. How you whisper-chant her name,

call her to you when she's already in your arms,
ask the ancestors for help when you struggle with loving her.

Trembling with it, needing to be a bigger container.
Scared that someday she'll say

You made us both too small.

Facts about Yellow

The sun is white, but speaks yellow.
Explosions in the sun birth particles
called neutrinos. So small they pass
through our cells. There's often a cost
for not feeling something, a biological tax
due later. But in this case, our insides
are lit with tiny bits of sun, and it's ok.
Though plants are sun eaters, houseplants
yellow in the dark. The toddler's missing
scarf is yellow too. As are the trash cans,
golden fossils, announcing that a reckless sky
has set itself on fire again. Late afternoon
in December and the air is liquid amber—ecstatic,
you can tell—even though you never get outside
before the houses swallow the sun, and you're
trying to remember the last time you weren't
tired. And doesn't everything hinge on this:
the yellow grass revealed by thaw, crooked
and tender, and something older than mercy,
never unmoving, a yellow square sliding across
the floor and halfway up the wall as we tip
towards a longer dark.

Facts about Gravity
for Joke

It's everywhere,

      decreases with distance while never fully arriving at zero.

      Orbits are born of perfect symmetry between

a body's forward motion and the tug of gravity from

      another body. Gravity plays tetherball with galaxies.

      The week we knew you were leaving,

    gravity set snowflakes along electrical

wires, offered them to the trees to collect and carry

      like bright goblets on a windless day.

Quantum equations fall apart when they try

      to include gravity. The science of the very small,

irreconcilable with the weight of your hand.

      All things with mass or energy

gravitate towards one another—the earth

      meeting us after every leap.

But it's more complicated.

Gravitational fields bend the light of millions of suns.

Revolving celestial bodies twist the fabric

of the universe around themselves like

spaghetti around a fork, and I don't pretend

to understand much of this, but I can say that the day

you unfastened from your body, the earth did not

fling us outward as it spun.

After 41 days and nights orbiting your bedside,

I didn't fall apart in the wake of your death, except

for when I did,

and because time and space are not absolute,

the universe built not of things, but of happenings—

a twist of interrelated events—you haven't

stopped happening.

And because gravity shapes the medium

        through which sound travels, I still speak to you, held

and changed by your presence.

        By the fact of a body's weight, reduced

to fistfuls of ash, given to the river, borne along

        by the current.

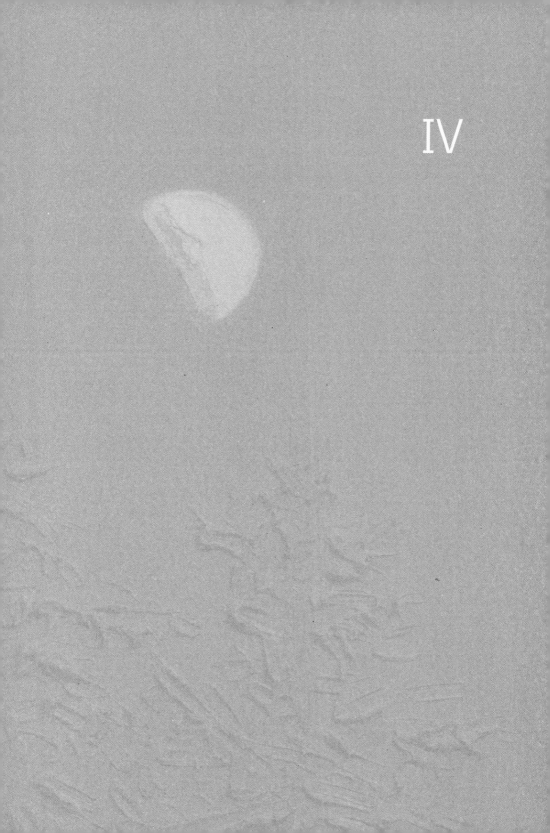

IV

Field Guide

for Sophie

The 2020 edition of the *Field Guide to Grief*
covers a wide range of sorrows. Chapters
on bushfires, locusts, coping with a culture
that wants you to get over it in six months.
Oddly specific passages: What to say
into the silence after you ask for a shovel,
having arrived trembling at a dinner party,
the still-warm body of the fox you just ran over
seeping red onto your arms. An expanded
section on grieving while parenting—the toddler
who imitates your laugh, doesn't know
the difference between laughing and crying:
HAW HAW HAW whenever you crumple
on the kitchen floor. Then, of course,
mourning in quarantine. How to touch each
other when we cannot touch each other.
How to gather the river in both hands.
What I'm trying to say is I can't believe
you overdosed at the start of a pandemic.
Two days earlier I was still shaking
people's hands. Then we sat through your
memorial with our hands in our laps,
still thinking that could keep us safe.

The Cooper's Hawk That Had a Meal

and the slick red breastbone inside a ring of feathers on snow.
All the birds and their tree clamour. The silver maple
at Jackson and Grange, its wide roots swallowing the sidewalk.
The toddler insisting I stop the stroller right next to it.
Nightly wakings. Hours of humming "The Little Drummer Boy"
until her breathing slows and I pull her, limp and warm,
over my torso. The heart beating an inch from mine
before I sit up and set her back in her crib. The garbage
truck we chase on Tuesdays, her shriek each time
the metal arms grab, lift, and shake. A sudden rain,
the storm drain's echo and clatter as it sucks back cigarette butts,
leaves, a dead mouse, rain. An empty playground.
Everyone standing six feet apart in line at the grocery store.
Houseplants dropping dry husks on the carpet.
The body, not sick, just too tired to regulate
temperature—cold and hot and cold again. The body,
somehow still anchored by all that continues
even while so much must stop.

On Day 22 I Learn My Little Brother Has Covid

The toddler doesn't understand when I cry
so we try drawing. When the last crayon

clatters to the floor, I choose a knife
and cut open a lemon. I've seen the videos

so I try not to laugh as I lick a bright slice
and offer it to her. She steps close, her breath

damp on my cheek. Pauses the way she does
with newness, feeling around inside for

a *Yes/No/Wait*. Dips her mouth to the curve
of my favourite fruit. Her face twists

and she pauses then taps her fingers together
to make the sign for *More*. It becomes

a game: turn by turn, sitting on the kitchen
floor watching each other touch tongues

to yellow flesh. Forty minutes pass.
God is the cool sour moon we hand back

and forth, setting teeth into it just once.

Permission

The stinging nettle patch behind the house
greens earlier than roadside or river

nettle. A romantic gesture from a partner
who planted them for me even though

he fears the sting, wears thick gloves
to gather them for tea, gets nervous in late

summer when the entire nettle patch leans out
tall and heavy over the walkway. But that comes

later. This morning they were barely four inches.
Urtica dioica. Little poem of a name: burn of two

houses. I finally looked up the pronunciation.
Dye-OH-ick-a. Hot ancient hum on my bare hands

at harvesting taught me to ask permission.
May I take some? May I take more?

Thank you. Keeper of the good fire, green-
arrowed signature written into wet earth,

each year since moving back I've said *This might
be the most beautiful spring yet* and I said it

again this May, and meant it, despite everything,
despite it being the first spring I'd rubbed nettle

on skin, seeking the sting—*May I?*—just
to feel something.

Good News
for Anna

Oh, frogs, that's good news,
my therapist said. I knew what she meant,
how frogs drink and breathe through
their skin. But I wonder if it really means
the stream is healthy. What if the frogs
are sick, barely hanging on? I didn't
say that. Did you know about
the glass frogs in the Amazon?
Those rice-sized crimson hearts
knocking at the window of their chests.
Of course they're endangered.
Still, as soon as I read it, I made a note
to tell you. Shit is hard. I don't know
when I'll see you again. I want
to hold each thing that deepens
the well. That's what we want to tell
each other, isn't it? The skin, eyelid-
thin, ribs no longer a cage, and the joy,
rising to meet what's next.
To find out if it's good news.

Trespassing Again at the Everton Cascade

Mud sucks at my ankles. I stand up to my hips
in a misfit stream—a river too wide

or too narrow to have eroded the passage
in which it flows. Forever too much or not enough.

The forest above me, pocked with bowls
and cylindrical shafts where ice water flung rocks,

lodged them in bedrock. Drilling. Carving columns
with the rush and force of water.

It must have been so loud for so long.
There are people I love who might die

before it's safe for us to touch again. This is only
my pain, unless it's yours too. The water, just hip deep.

I wish to be more present—don't we all?
For something other than regret as anchor.

But if the river is the suture that grief seeps around,
why not throw in all my limbs,

scatter the crayfish, then climb out to breathe
and drip on the shore.

Echolocation

It clouds over as soon as I lie down in a field at the Jesuit centre.
A blur of bats wing above in the overcast gloom, bouncing

sound off insects, trees. Attuned to the symmetry of their own
returning voice. It's twilight during the Perseids meteor showers.

I try to grasp how space and time are the interconnected
fabric of the universe, or how our every atom

originated from the flaming gaseous core of a star,
but I keep getting distracted by potential metaphors.

I'm letting go of everyone who loved me once but doesn't
anymore. It's not sad. For one leaping moment I see bright

movement behind a thin patch of cloud. It's just a plane.
If I hardly have time to see my friends anymore,

and we can't touch when I do, am I a different person?
Everything I write contains now this distance.

The pitch and tilt of it like a field where I sing out to the dark
to learn where I am, while bats eat mosquitos

that have bitten me, my blood moving and warm in us all.

Day 217

Fifty or more, yanking at grass
with their bills, tearing it free
with quick jerks. The curve

of their backs gleam bright
enough to hurt the eyes. Shadows
yawn across the frozen ground.

There will be a rise
in suicides this winter, I told
a friend last night.

Another five or ten geese
sweep in and the toddler cries, *Maw, maw.*
More, more. I'll wash green smears

from her jeans tonight.
The geese puff chests, beat
wings, scold their neighbours. Settle,

graze, repeat. I envy them their proximity
to one other. The internet gives risk
statistics. *Only you can know*

what's right for your family. We share lists
of ways to get through winter. People
talk about the "after times." I watch

a short film, *The Years of Repair,*
sob into my palms at the kitchen table.
Hope crouches low to the ground. Wails

if anything touches it. In two weeks,
the election. In two weeks, a full moon.
The toddler can't make the "oo" sound yet,

will shout, *Meen, meen,* on our morning
walk, demand that I pick her up, wanting
to get closer to it before it slips down

behind the houses. Yesterday the trees
let go a thousand shades of orange,
butter, lemon, burgundy, casting circles

of colour along Farquhar Street.
The sweet smell of rot.
I sat on the curb listening

to the *tsh, tsh* of dropping leaves,
every tender landing, the maples
chanting, *death, death, death.*

Waiting for Owls

Dev's been visiting the screech owls
since last winter. She'd sit in the snow with a Caesar

and stare up at the dead snag. Waiting
for them to fly out of the cavity at dusk.

They swooped low enough to skim the ground,
made whinnying cries like owl-sized ponies.

My eyes do that thing when I look
at something for too long; the edges of the dead tree

glow, almost pink against an overcast sky.
I read that a barred owl shot in New England

had a long-eared owl in its stomach
which had a screech owl in its stomach.

I want it to be true. If I could climb the tree,
peer inside, would I see them nestled close?

Ghost owl, demon owl, dusk owl, mouse owl.
When owls swallow prey whole, they eat it head first

so the feet slip down the right way.
With owl vision I could predict their nighttime

emergence based on puffs of breath just above the opening.
We speak low without looking away from the tree.

Dev says sometimes they just appear in a different tree,
as if by teleportation. What a relief to bring all of me

here, the insistent cold at my feet. Waiting
on an event that might not happen.

Willing to be limp in the claws of it for a moment.

Ode to the Ampersand

Its loop & curl, the sleek belly, the invitation to continue. The poetry editor pained by it & every writing manual cautioning against its overuse. The former 27th letter of the alphabet, too awkward to name at the end of the tune & cast off like a vestigial tail (reminiscent of Pluto's demotion to dwarf planet status for its lack of gravitational pull, unable to empty its orbital neighbourhood of debris). Its beginnings as a ligature, built of pieces fused together, & the root word leig, meaning to tie or to bind—like thread in surgery, or obligation. Being joyfully bound to all that I love, including the grief pulling me to the floor, & the small things which turn inside grief like rocks in a tumbler. The Covid mourning ritual last month, the labyrinth of string lights we entered to kneel at the centre. Wet grass & heavy rain. The dark paths & surging black of the river. Absent streetlights. Another winter of seeing friends only outdoors, & the sunny spot on the carpet where I go to wail. Making a meal of this. An ordinary habit. Just grief & me, sitting in a field. Nothing to talk about.

Facts about Coyotes

for Dave

Coyotes run on tiptoe when they want to be quiet,
can leap a distance of 13 feet.

Once, I woke to a group yip-howl, body blooming
with goosebumps. Went back to sleep promising to remember.

Coyotes bark, yip, and howl. They warble, lilt,
and trill. Modulate and inflect with lips and tongues.

Once, on a full moon we heard a young coyote—
the five-year-old across the street praising the moon

from the porch. I scooped up the toddler
and we howled back from the driveway.

Two months into the pandemic, musicians paraded down
the sidewalk playing accordion and clarinet. People

spilled out of their houses. You, me, the toddler, the neighbours
two doors down, the folks opposite us. Six feet apart and beaming.

Coyotes devour rattlesnakes, porcupines, and garbage. They're hard
to get rid of. Poison, traps, guns, and hunting dogs haven't worked.

A week later, the house opposite us caught fire.
The man who lives there said *Everything's fine*, but his wife—

who I'd never seen—yelled from within, *Call 911*.
We stayed outside, remember, because of the sirens,

the smoke billowing from the kitchen window, but also, to see
each other's faces. Our friends can't enter our homes,

there's not enough air in here, and it hurts.
A relocated coyote will do whatever it takes to get back home.

The morning after the howling woke me, I stepped
over coyote shit on the front step. I want to think

we're closer than we know. Close as a house fire,
as live music. Only as far as the next portal to a shared *yes*.

Yes to the moon, to the accordion and clarinet,
calling the fire truck, calling each other's kids off the road.

Yes to love poems, and pointing out every murmuration
rippling across a winter sky. Yes to running up to you

on tiptoes just because I can, love. Changed and uncareful
and so goddamn happy to see you.

Acknowledgements

Gratitude to the following publications and organizations who published poems from this collection.

"An Alternate Universe in Which My Trauma Responses Are Made of Birds." *Rogue Agent*, Issue 96, March 2023.
"Echolocation," "Permission." *Canthius,* February 2022.
"Explanation," "If You Sing It Slowly Enough," "Ode to the Mississauga Women's Clinic," "She Says It's Dangerous to Open Umbrellas Indoors." *EVENT*, 51/2, 2022.
"Facts about Coyotes," "Waiting for Owls." *CV2*, vol. 45 no. 4, April 2023.
"Facts about Gravity." *Human & Nature*, Spring 2025.
"Facts about Yellow," "In Defence of Purple," "Trespassing Again at the Everton Cascade." *Riddle Fence*, Issue 41, August 2021.
"Field Guide." CBC Poetry Prize longlist 2020
"How to Win after Leaving." *Vagabond City*, January 2023.
"It Is Relevant That I'm Ovulating." *PRISM*, Issue 60.1, Fall 2021.
"Poem That Wanted to Be an Apple." *Pinhole Poetry*, July 2023.
"The Mouth Is Your Hardest and Softest Place." *untethered magazine*, vol. 14, June 2023.
"Time Machine," "When Whales Went Back to the Water." *swifts & slows*, June 2023.

Creation of this work was funded in part by an Ontario Arts Council grant and a Canada Council for the Arts grant.
The titles of "Poem That Wanted to Be an Apple" and "Poem That Wanted to Be an Icicle" are based on a title construction by William Stobb.

The titles of "Facts about Gravity," "Facts about Coyotes," and "Facts about Yellow" are based on a title construction by Mindy Nettifee.

I wrote this book mostly in small intervals while the toddler slept. First and foremost my thanks to little K for lighting up my life on the regular, and for being a reliable napper in the early pandemic years. Thanks also to Dave for supporting me to carve out time and space for poetry, and for continuing to inspire love poems. Thanks to Anna for the poetry editing dates that shaped and fed this book (may we think and write and marvel together for all of our lives).

Thank you to the many excellent editors who helped to hone some or many of these poems: Gil Adamson, Michelle Lobkowicz, Buddy Wakefield, Megan Falley, Shira Erlichman, Leah Horlick, Adèle Barclay, Anna Bowen, the two anonymous jurors at University of Alberta Press, and especially Jeanann Verlee and Anna Swanson.

Thank you to Maureen Blackwood and Lisa Rohleder for being my first listeners, always ready to hear a new poem.

Thank you to Chris Lafazanos and Amelia Meister for celebrating poetry month with me every April and witnessing many suspect first drafts.

Thank you to Charlie Petch for the sensitivity reading of the second section of this book. Any mistakes or oversights are mine.

Thank you to Ziysah von Bieberstein, Marie Metaphor Specht, Hannah Renglich, Lishai Peel and Jeremy Loveday for the online poetry gatherings—I still loathe zoom but I love being with all of you.

Thank you to Dev Ridge for teaching me about birds.

Thank you to the University of Alberta Press team for saying yes to this book, for helping me make it better, and for the professionalism and warmth. This process has been a delight.

These poems were written in Thadinadonnih ("the place
where they built"), which is the territory of the Attawandaron/
Chonnonton/Neutral and the Haudenosaunee peoples, the treaty
land of the Mississaugas of the Credit First Nation, and is
governed by the Dish with One Spoon covenant. (Also known as
Guelph, Ontario. Also known more broadly as Canada. Also
known as an ongoing project of genocide, land theft, and erasure,
some of which has always been accomplished through word
craft, which is worth mentioning in a book of poetry.)